JOSEPH LIEBERMAN

JOSEPH LIEBERMAN

BARBARA SILBERDICK FEINBERG

A Gateway Biography
The Millbrook Press
Brookfield, Connecticut

Published by The Millbrook Press, Inc.
2 Old New Milford Road
Brookfield, Connecticut 06804
www.millbrookpress.com

Library of Congress Cataloging-in-Publication Data
Feinberg, Barbara Silberdick.
Joseph Lieberman : keeping the faith / Barbara Jane Feinberg.
    p. cm. — (A Gateway biography)
Includes bibliographical references and index.
ISBN 0-7613-2303-1 (lib. bdg.)
1. Lieberman, Joseph I.—Juvenile literature. 2. Legislators—United States—
Biography—Juvenile literature. 3. United States. Congress. Senate—
Biography—Juvenile literature. 4. Vice-Presidential candidates—United
States—Biography—Juvenile literature. [1. Lieberman, Joseph I. 2. Vice-
Presidential candidates. 3. Legislators.] I. Title. II. Series.
E840.8.L46 F45 2001 973.929'092—dc21 [B] 00-066429

Cover photograph courtesy of Liaison Agency (© Chuck Kennedy)

Photographs courtesy of © AFP/CORBIS: pp. 6, 39, 40; Senator Joseph
Lieberman: pp. 9, 15; CNP/Archive Photos: pp. 11, 21, 31; AP/Wide World
Photos: pp. 17, 22, 25, 26, 34, 37, 38, 41, 43, 44; Reuters/Mike Segar/Archive
Photos: p. 32

CONTENTS

GROWING UP

America gives you the freedom to be what you are.

Joseph Isador Lieberman was born on February 24, 1942, in Stamford, Connecticut, a coastal city then numbering almost 48,000 people. His hardworking neighbors included Irish, Germans, Italians, Poles, African Americans, and Jews. Stamford children respected one another's differences. In the 1940s and 1950s, the city had only one public high school for all of them. According to Joe's childhood friend Joe Richichi, "Here you had Joe's dad, being Jewish, and my dad, the Italian barber, and right next door was Burns Tavern. Joe saw no color. Joe saw no differences in religion."

Joe's parents, Marcia and Henry Lieberman, were born in America. Their parents were Jews who came from Austria and Poland in the early 1900s. Henry Lieberman spent his childhood in an orphanage. Marcia was one of five children raised by a wid-

Joseph Lieberman, the first Jewish American to be nominated for vice president, accepts the Democratic nomination during the Democratic National Convention in Los Angeles, California, in August 2000.

owed mother, Minnie Manger. Henry and Marcia met at a dance at the Jewish Center in Stamford and married in 1940. To earn a living, Henry Lieberman drove a bakery truck for eighteen dollars a week. Then in 1940, he opened his own liquor store.

For the first eight years of his life, Joe and his parents lived with his grandmother Minnie. Their home was in a run-down neighborhood near the railroad tracks. On one side was junkyard. Yet Joe did not feel threatened or unhappy. His neighborhood was seedy, not dangerous. Then the Liebermans moved to a house on Strawberry Hill Court, where Joe's mother still lives.

As a child, Joe developed a sense of responsibility and a desire to succeed. His grandmother's stories, the teachings of his religion, and his father's example shaped his character. He wrote that his grandmother Minnie "was a heroic figure to me." She had come to Stamford from a small Eastern European village where she had been mistreated because of her religion. In Stamford, she was accepted and respected for who she was. From her stories, Joe learned about the difficulties of life in Europe and the blessings of freedom in the United States.

The Liebermans were observant Jews. This meant that they kept a kosher home by only eating food that was made according to Jewish dietary laws. They had separate sets of dishes for meat and dairy foods. They honored the Sabbath by not working or doing household chores from Friday at sundown until Saturday at sundown. They also had to walk to temple to say their prayers because traveling in cars or buses was not permitted.

Henry and Marcia Lieberman help their son, Joseph, stand on the porch railing of their home in Stamford, Connecticut.

Joe has stated that his parents encouraged him to openly accept the Jewish faith. "They had a real belief that America gives you the freedom to be what you are and that preserving your unique heritage contributes to the strength and the diversity of the country." As Jews, Joe's parents believed that life is a gift from God and that everyone should serve God by helping the community. The Liebermans passed this belief on to their son and to their daughters, Rietta and Ellen, Joe's younger sisters. Thus it is not surprising that as a child, Joe tried to make himself useful to others.

From his father, Joe learned the values of love of country and hard work. Joe has written, "Pop was a quiet man, but he spoke to us clearly with his actions." Like other able-bodied American men, Henry Lieberman served in the U.S. Army during World War II. Young Joe missed his father so much that he stuttered for the year that his father was away. From 1941 to 1945, the United States was fighting against Nazi Germany and Fascist Italy in Europe and against militaristic Japan in Asia.

Henry had never gone to college, but education was important to him. When he came home from the war, he spent long hours working at the liquor store. Joe remembered how his father would read literature and philosophy when business was slow. The radio was on all the time, tuned to a classical music station. Through hard work, he eventually earned enough money to give his children college educations.

Joe feared failure. He desperately wanted to succeed. He was so nervous before baseball games that sometimes he even threw up.

Joe steps up to bat for the Stamford Fire Department Little League team.

Jack Romanos played with Joe in Little League. He remembered that Joe was sent to play in deep right field where he couldn't get hurt. "I joke with Joe that he learned pretty quickly that athletics were not going to be his way to fame and fortune. He was awful." He would never play for the New York Yankees, but he became a lifelong fan.

Joe discovered that his people skills were much better than his athletic skills. According to a summer camp counselor, nine-year-old Joe came up with a plan to build a miniature golf course as part of an arts and crafts project. "He got all the kids to work together to build this course."

Joe became interested in politics in 1951. That year the Senate Crime Investigation Committee led by Senator Estes Kefauver of Tennessee held televised hearings. The committee investigated the connections between politics and organized crime in major cities. Joe was fascinated watching the "good guys" scold the "bad guys." The next year, he stayed up to see the presidential election results. His grandmother supported the victorious Republican candidate, General Dwight D. Eisenhower. His parents had preferred the Democratic governor of Illinois, Adlai E. Stevenson.

When Joe entered Stamford High School in 1956, he was a member of a minority group. However, he never experienced anti-Semitism, hostile feelings toward Jews. Joe recalled, "Most of my friends were not Jewish, but it was a wonderful, open, respectful community." He was elected class president in the ninth-grade. In his campaign speech he used the titles of popular rock and roll songs to call attention to his message. During the next three years he found time to join the choir, the debating society, and his temple's youth group. He was elected class president again in his senior year. Teacher Herman Alswanger recalled, "I remember him [saying] that he wanted the political life. He said his goal and dream would be [to become] a senator."

Joe took his responsibilities as a leader very seriously. According to his mother, he and his friends tutored students in her living room. The students lacked enough credits to graduate, and Stamford had no summer school then. As more and more children came to the Liebermans for help, the principal told Joe, "Go to the school cupboards and take whatever you need—all the reading material and books you need, and you can meet in the high school."

Joe was chosen to be prom king that year. He did not attend the dance, because it was held on a Saturday, the Jewish Sabbath. He remained true to his religious beliefs. He had learned to make choices between what he would like to do and what was expected of him. He soon would face other challenges at Yale University.

Studying at Yale

[I]t is usually better to compromise and make progress than to remain inflexible.

Joe was under pressure to succeed when he came to Yale University in 1960. He admitted, "I had a rocky time with my classes the first semester." He was the first member of his family to go to college, and he wanted to make his parents proud of him. Also, he was from a public high school, and he was surrounded by students from prep schools. Their education had more depth than his. In addition, he was a Jew. Yale still had unofficial admissions quotas, limiting the number of Jews to 10 percent of the student body. In college, Joe abandoned religious observance for a time. "Like any kid, I left it for a while—to experience sin, but I missed it," he explained with a smile.

By his second year, his grades improved, and Joe threw himself into campus life. He was inspired by President John F. Kennedy's appeal to the nation: "Ask not what your country can do for you. Ask what you can do for your country." Joe was elected class treasurer, and he joined the staff of the *Yale Daily News*. There was no student government, so the campus newspaper was the center of college political life.

Lieberman, left, received his undergraduate degree from Yale University in 1964.

During staff meetings, Joe used his people skills to help reporters with differing political beliefs find ideas they could agree on. For example, campus custodians and food-service workers demanded better working conditions and higher pay. Joe supported the workers' demands. Classmate Jon M. Van Dyke commented, "Most of us considered this an annoyance. To him, the working man was sort of the paradigm [example] that we all should support."

In 1962, Joe became chairman and chief editorial writer of the *News*. As chairman, he met once a week with the president of Yale University, Kingman Brewster Jr. Both men wanted Yale to admit women to the all-male campus. They also wanted to end unofficial quotas that limited the admission of minorities. In 1962, Joe was also selected to join the Elihu secret society, a Yale social club.

During the summer of 1963, he worked in the office of Democratic Senator Abraham Ribicoff of Connecticut, a Jew. "And he taught me . . . that it is usually better to compromise and make progress than to remain inflexible."

That summer, Joe took part in Dr. Martin Luther King Jr.'s March on Washington. Throughout the 1960s, the civil-rights movement focused attention on the unjust treatment of blacks in the South. Joe had already expressed his opinion in emotional editorials in the school paper urging an end to racial prejudice.

Joe was also a strong supporter of free speech. In the fall of 1963, a group of Yale students invited Governor George Wallace of Alabama to speak on campus. Wallace forcefully opposed equal

More than 200,000 Americans, including Joseph Lieberman, joined Martin Luther King Jr.'s March on Washington in August 1963.

treatment of blacks, so President Brewster canceled the invitation. Joe thought Brewster was wrong to censor the governor, and, according to a *News* staffer, he "raked Brewster over the coals" in the paper. Even though Joe disagreed with Wallace, he thought Wallace had the right to speak. To Joe, his values were more important than his relationship with the university president.

Joe was often quick to think and to write about problems but slow to act. In the fall of 1963 a group of Yale students planned a twenty-five-hour drive to Mississippi. They were going to teach black voters how to register. Ever since the 1880s, Southerners had rigged the laws and even resorted to terror to keep African Americans from voting. Initially, Joe wanted to stay on campus and write about the trip from his office at the *News*. However, Yale chaplain William Sloane Coffin and activist Allard Lowenstein, two popular civil-rights crusaders, convinced him to "go and lead and get other people to go." Joe went to Mississippi to help, but first he wrote an article in the college newspaper explaining his actions. "I am going to Mississippi because there is much work to be done there and few men are doing it."

The group saw firsthand the miserable conditions Southern African Americans endured. The Yale group faced problems, such as rocks stuffed in their gas tanks. However, they were in no real danger. Just a year later, conditions became much worse, and three college-age civil-rights workers were brutally murdered in Mississippi for helping blacks register to vote.

His last year in college, Joe's grades were so good that he was chosen for the Scholar of the House program. Instead of attending classes, he was expected to prepare a thesis, a long report. He decided to write about John M. Bailey of Connecticut, the Democratic state party chairman. Bailey was in charge of Democrats all over Connecticut. He was a professional politician, an old-style party boss who traded favors for power. Joe learned from him how important it was to get along and to be well organized. Joe was awarded the Frank M. Patterson Prize and $1,000 for his thesis. This flattering portrait of Bailey was published as a book, *The Power Broker*, in 1966.

The summer after his graduation in 1964, Joe Lieberman worked for Bailey at the Democratic National Committee, in Washington, D.C. Then he attended Yale Law School. He felt that law school "would help me be a better public official and would also provide an independent livelihood if my political career did not succeed."

In 1964, the United States officially became involved in the Vietnam War. For the next eleven years, the government tried to keep the Republic of South Vietnam from being taken over by the Communist North Vietnamese. At Yale, as well as on other college campuses, students protested the draft, the law that required people to join the armed services. They thought the United States should not interfere in a civil war between Vietnamese. "I was anti-war," Joe Lieberman claimed, but he took a while to make up his mind. Because he was a student, and later a parent, he was allowed to put off his required military service.

In 1965, he married Betty Haas, a social worker. She had been an intern in Senator Ribicoff's office in 1963. Their son, Matt, was born in 1967; their daughter, Rebecca, in 1969. Lieberman never did serve in the armed forces. Later, he expressed some regret about not helping fight in the Vietnam War. However, he had already set his sights on serving his community in another way: state politics.

SERVING IN STATE POLITICS

To help people on the Sabbath,
that overrides the normal prohibitions.

As a Yale Law School student, Lieberman wanted to run for alderman. (Aldermen are city officials.) However, he had not lived in New Haven long enough to qualify as a candidate. After graduating in 1967, he began to practice law in town. He also became the state chairman of Citizens for Kennedy, during Robert F. Kennedy's 1968 presidential campaign.

In 1970, his book *The Scorpion and the Tarantula* was published. It described early attempts and problems controlling the spread of nuclear weapons. That same year, Lieberman decided to run for state senator, to make laws for the state of Connecticut. He was starting at the top, rather than first seeking a local job, such as alderman, as was customary. Lieberman had learned that Ed Marcus, a powerful state senator, wanted to be the next U.S. senator from Connecticut. If Marcus did not succeed he planned to return to the state legislature. No Democrat was willing to challenge his claim to a state senate seat until Lieberman came along.

Democratic party boss John M. Bailey and Senator Abraham Ribicoff decided to support Lieberman. With their help, the twenty-eight-year-old lawyer managed to raise $30,000 for his campaign, an unheard-of amount for a challenger. Yale law student and future U.S. president Bill Clinton was one of many on campus who campaigned for Lieberman. They went door to door all over New Haven, asking people for their vote. Lieberman personally visited at least 3,000 homes. He won in 1970 by only 240 votes.

Lieberman celebrates with his supporters after his election to the Connecticut State Senate.

Lieberman put a lot of effort into each of his election campaigns, even the ones he lost.

As state senator, Lieberman championed liberal Democratic causes, including more aid to local schools, clean air and water, and women's rights. He served on the State and Urban Development Committee, working for state aid to central cities, like New Haven. Since being a state senator was a part-time job, Lieberman also worked for the New Haven Equal Opportunities Commission and became an assistant dean at Yale University.

In 1974, he was involved in Ella Grasso's successful campaign to become governor. That year Lieberman was chosen majority leader. (The party with the most seats in the legislature chooses the majority leader.) This gave Lieberman control of the agenda, the items to be presented for a Senate debate or a vote. According to one state official, Lieberman won the job because he had a gentle manner, was smart, and because "he was a listener." Governor Grasso was asked what she would do if the legislature had to meet during the majority leader's Sabbath. She replied, "If Joe has learned to live with his orthodoxy, we can learn to live with his orthodoxy."

In 1978, Lieberman wanted to become lieutenant governor, the official in charge when the governor was out of state or unable to serve. "I'd love to be governor some day and this would be a kind of training and preparation for the opportunity," he explained. Lieberman was unwilling to violate the Sabbath by attending the state Democratic convention. He lost the nomination to William O'Neill.

In 1980, Lieberman decided to run for the U.S. House of Representatives. Three weeks before Election Day, the polls showed him 19 percentage points ahead of his opponent, Larry De Nardis. So Lieberman stopped polling. He also failed to respond to political attacks on his record in state government. He lost, and these choices may have cost him the election. It was also the year Ronald Reagan became president and brought Republicans to power along with him.

Lieberman suffered another disappointment in 1981. His marriage to Betty Haas fell apart. He had gone back to the strict religious practices of his youth. His wife was not used to observing Jewish traditions. They tried marriage counseling, with little success, and then divorced. Under a shared custody agreement, the children spent half the week with each parent.

Things could only get better. In 1982, he published his book *The Legacy*. It traced Connecticut politics from 1930 to 1980. In 1982, Lieberman was elected attorney general of Connecticut. It was his job to bring lawsuits on behalf of the state and its citizens. As an observant Jew, Lieberman was not present on the Saturday the state Democratic party nominated him. He did not campaign on the Sabbath either, but he managed to perform his official duties. As he told reporters, "If you have an opportunity to help people on the Sabbath, that overrides the normal prohibitions. When I was attorney general, they always knew on a holy day they could call me for decisions or ask me to sign papers."

During his two terms (six years), Lieberman carried out his promise "to be the people's lawyer." He fought for clean air and clean water. He attacked supermarkets for fixing prices (forcing consumers to pay the same amount at any store). He accused gasoline companies and cable television companies of overcharging customers. He also went after parents who failed to pay child support. He issued a column of consumer tips, sent out to newspapers statewide. A Republican noted that "Joe raised the profile of the office—and at the same time raised the profile of Joe Lieberman."

Lieberman's wife, Hadassah, is one of his biggest supporters.

Joe Lieberman flew to Florida to surprise his mother on her eighty-sixth birthday while she was helping him campaign. After phoning her from backstage to wish her a happy birthday, Joe walked onstage with a dozen red roses.

Meanwhile, in 1982, he met Hadassah (Esther) Freilich Tucker, a divorcée with a seven-year-old son, Ethan. Her parents had survived the Holocaust, a time from the late 1930s to 1945 when the Nazi Germans forced Jews to leave their homes, imprisoned them in concentration camps, enslaved them, and murdered them. After the war, the Freilichs moved to Czechoslovakia. Hadassah came to the United States as an infant in 1949, when the Communists took over that country. Her father served as a rabbi in the small town of Gardner, Massachusetts. With a master's degree in American government and international relations, she was working as a public-relations consultant when she married Lieberman in 1983.

In 1986, Henry Lieberman died. Joe Lieberman wrote a ten-page tribute to his father, noting: "Strength, Principle, Civility. These are his legacies to us. These were his ideals." His mother remained in the family home on Strawberry Hill Court. Mother and son remained close. He phoned her daily and sent her out as his unofficial spokesperson to senior citizens. She was delighted by the arrival of Hadassah and Joe's child, her new granddaughter, Hana, in 1988. That was also the year her son decided to run for the United States Senate.

Becoming a U.S. Senator

I am going to do what I think is right on every issue.

In 1988, Joe Lieberman decided to challenge Republican Lowell Weicker for his seat in the U.S. Senate. The senator had served three terms (18 years) and looked unbeatable. For months, polls showed Lieberman losing to him.

Then, late in the campaign, Lieberman's team ran a cartoon advertisement on TV that depicted Weicker as a sleepy bear. The bear napped during important Senate votes and woke up only when something mattered to him personally. This was the first negative television ad campaign in Connecticut history. It helped Lieberman win an upset victory—by just 10,000 votes. When he ran for reelection six years later, he beat his opponent, Jerry Labriola, by more than 350,000 votes, the largest victory in a Connecticut senate election.

The Liebermans had moved to the nation's capital, but they were not active on the social scene. They liked quiet dinners with friends better than large Washington parties. The couple reveled in their family life. "There is nothing like coming home and changing a baby's diaper to remind you that being a senator is just your job," the senator wrote. Hadassah Lieberman worked part-time so she could devote herself to the children and her husband.

Lieberman had to balance the demands of his religion with his Senate duties. On the Sabbath, when he was needed at the Capitol, he walked $4\frac{1}{2}$ miles (7.25 kilometers) from his home in Georgetown. He cast some seventy-five votes by voice instead of by pressing the electric buttons, as most senators did. He planned to sleep on a cot in the Senate gym if he had to stay late to vote on a Sabbath night.

However, Al Gore, then a Tennessee senator, had a better idea. "My mother and father live across the street, and they're away right now. Come on over," he offered. Gore put on the lights and got things ready for Lieberman, knowing that on the Sabbath he was forbidden to do these things himself. Pauline Gore, the senator's mother, continues to call Lieberman "her tenant." Out of respect for Senator Lieberman's religion, the Senate no longer meets on High Holy Days, and no votes are taken on Jewish festival days.

In 1989, Republican George Bush was president, and the Democratic party controlled Congress. Lieberman was a newcomer who supported bipartisanship, cooperation between the two parties. "To me the best way to get things done in this government or in this country is to . . . work across party lines when you agree." He voted with his party on measures for clean air and water, the right of a woman to end an unwanted pregnancy, gun control, protecting consumers, civil-rights laws, and welfare reforms.

He disagreed with most Democrats by supporting school vouchers. Vouchers give parents the right to use government funds to send their children to schools of their choice. Lieberman's children attended private schools in the Washington area. The senator voted for experimental projects that let parents take children out of the worst public schools and send them elsewhere. His stand offended public school teachers' unions.

He also opposed affirmative action (setting aside jobs, contracts, or school placements for minorities). Blacks were not pleased with his position. As a Jew subjected to a religious quota at Yale, however, he could not support programs that seemed to impose quotas based on race, religion, or any other differences among people. He did believe in equal opportunity and programs to give people a chance to improve themselves.

There were other issues where he broke with his party and sided with the Republicans. In 1991 he was one of ten Democrats voting to send American troops to fight in the Gulf War, to remove Iraqi troops from Kuwait. He also favored the 1991 Supreme Court nomination of Republican Clarence Thomas, a Yale Law School graduate. Thomas was a conservative African-American lawyer. However, like most Democrats, Lieberman voted against him after a former coworker accused Thomas of harassing her.

Senator Lieberman protected his state's defense, insurance, and drug industries. For example, as a member of the Armed Services

During the Persian Gulf War, Senator Lieberman visits U.S. troops in Saudi Arabia.

Committee, he backed the Connecticut-based building of Sea Wolf submarines and Blackhawk and Comanche helicopters. He was more enthusiastic about military spending than most Democrats. He even endorsed the sale of jet fighter planes to Israel's traditional foe Saudi Arabia.

Lieberman helps during Bill Clinton's presidential campaign.

He also protected insurance companies from a proposed $7 billion tax package. On the other hand, he supported a strong patient bill of rights the insurers did not want. Lieberman stood up to the drug companies when he thought they were wrong. He opposed the high prices they charged for prescriptions.

In 1992, Lieberman was pleased when Bill Clinton and Al Gore were elected U.S. president and vice president. Earlier, he had joined them on the Democratic Leadership Council (DLC). It was a "think tank" that developed new ideas to improve the party. The DLC recommended such programs as increasing trade with other countries and cutting the size of the federal government to make the economy grow. Lieberman became chairman of the DLC in 1995.

He was known as the "conscience of the Senate." As Lieberman explained, "I am going to do what I think is right on every issue." He did not let his friendships with the president and vice president affect his judgment or his actions. In 1997, he was a member of a committee investigating the way President Clinton and Vice President Gore raised money for their 1996 presidential re-election campaign.

Unlike other Democrats on the committee, Lieberman asked witnesses tough questions. Republicans argued that Clinton and Gore should not have raised money by inviting guests to the White House for coffee in exchange for campaign contributions. Using the president's official home and office for fund-raising gave them an unfair advantage over their opponents. Lieberman said, "I think those coffees were wrong. . . . I don't see evidence that they were illegal." In February 1998, he introduced a bill that forbade presidential candidates from personally raising funds for their campaigns, but the Senate did not pass any campaign reforms in 1998.

Lieberman with his granddaughters, Tennessee and Willie (asleep), and friends walking home from services at the temple.

In 1998, the House of Representatives impeached President Bill Clinton. In effect, they formally charged him with personal misconduct. He had had a relationship with a young woman who was not his wife. To make matters worse, he lied about it. Once the House voted to impeach, the Senate had to act as a court and decide whether or not to remove the president from office. This was a requirement of the U.S. Constitution.

Lieberman was the first Democrat to speak up in the Senate. The heartbroken, angry senator gave a speech condemning the president. "Such behavior is not just inappropriate. It is immoral. And it is harmful, for it sends a message of what is acceptable behavior to the larger American family, particularly to our children." After Lieberman's speech, other Democrats denounced the president's behavior, too. Unlike the Republicans, they did not think it was necessary to remove him from office. In fact, the Republicans did not have enough votes to force him out.

Lieberman's concern with moral conduct, with issues of right and wrong, also led him to join forces with the conservative former Secretary of Education William J. Bennett in 1998. They gave out Silver Sewer Awards to publicize the need to protect children from the violence, drug use, and sex found in many films, television shows, video games, and music, like "gangsta rap." The senator also pushed for a vee chip, an electronic device to block inappropriate television programs. He was campaigning to make entertainment safe for children. Little did he know that he would soon be campaigning for election as vice president of the United States.

CAMPAIGNING TO BE VICE PRESIDENT

*"What will we dream for our country, and
how will we make it come true?"*

On August 7, 2000, at 7 A.M., the Liebermans' alarm clock automatically turned on the television set. Joe Lieberman woke up to unexpected news. He heard that he was presidential candidate Al Gore's choice as a running mate. At the age of fifty-eight, Lieberman would become the first Jew selected as the vice presidential candidate of a major political party.

A little later, Gore phoned him to make a formal offer. As the stunned senator told the press, "The vice president asked me if I would do him the honor of running with him, and I said, 'Believe me, it's my honor.' I am humbled, I'm grateful, and I'm excited because I believe in you."

The Liebermans flew to Gore's campaign headquarters in Nashville, Tennessee, for the official announcement. The senator kept using words like *honored*, *exciting*, and *miraculous* over and over to describe his feelings. In the speech he gave at the Nashville War Memorial, Lieberman praised Al Gore for his courage in naming him. He also shared with the audience a conversation he had with the Reverend Jesse Jackson, the black civil-rights leader.

Vice President Al Gore and Senator Joe Lieberman at a rally announcing Lieberman as Gore's running mate

"He said to me, you know, Joe, each time a barrier falls for one person, the doors of opportunity open wider for every other American." Lieberman felt that he was truly living the American dream.

Lieberman referred to his partnership with Al Gore as the "American dream team." He used this theme again in Los Angeles, where he addressed the Democratic convention on

Lieberman addressing the Democratic National Convention . . .

. . . and debating political issues with Secretary Dick Cheney, the Republican candidate for vice president

Joe and Hadassah Lieberman during the 2000 election campaign

August 16. (Every four years, the political parties hold conventions to agree on a platform, or set of positions on the issues, and to approve the party's presidential and vice presidential candidates.) Lieberman stated, "The great question this year is, what will we dream for our country and how will we make it come true?" He urged Americans to break down the barriers and differences that still divide them so that everyone could realize his or her dreams for a better future. Lieberman reminded his audience that "only in America" was this possible.

Lieberman and Gore were running against Republican Governor George W. Bush of Texas and former Defense Secretary Richard Cheney. The competing candidates made public appearances, gave speeches, and debated the issues to convince voters to

In the back row: Matt, Rebecca, and Hana Lieberman cheer for their father with Kristin and Tipper Gore (in front) during his vice presidential campaign.

support them on Election Day. Everywhere Senator Lieberman campaigned, the crowds shouted "Go Joe Go!" He praised President Clinton's achievements.

Lieberman was criticized, however, for talking too much about religion. He defended himself by saying that he wanted to remind people of their faith. For him, people of all religions were "children of the same God." Their faith was a source of good conduct. It could help fight the vulgarity and violence in American life. It could help government in trying "to create a good society." He acknowledged, though, that unbelievers could be good, moral people, too.

Lieberman made the rounds of television talk shows, answering questions from interviewers. He told them that he still planned to run for his Senate seat in Connecticut. The senator was frequently asked how, if elected, he would handle his policy differences with Gore. For example, Lieberman had voted for school vouchers while Gore had opposed them. The senator pointed out that while they differed on this issue, they both wanted to improve schools. He patiently explained that "on matters like this, Al and I will have full and open debate in private, but when he decides, I'm with him." In private, Lieberman did not plan to be a "yes man," but in public he would always support the president's decisions.

According to the Constitution, the vice president leads the Senate and casts a deciding vote if there is a tie. Modern vice presidents also sit in on meetings and give the president advice. They also chair government commissions. As vice president, Al Gore

Lieberman returns to Connecticut to celebrate his reelection to the Senate.

headed one such group that studied ways to make the government work better. Vice presidents travel abroad, representing the nation. Historically, their most important job has been to step up to the presidency if the elected president dies in office.

With this in mind, reporters asked Lieberman how he would handle his duties as vice president on the Sabbath. The candidate answered that "when you have a responsibility to people that can

Joe and Hadassah Lieberman laugh with former running-mate Al Gore during a rehearsal of the Senate swearing-in ceremony.

protect or advance their well-being or their lives, then you have got to do it." He added that the Sabbath was a day of rest to honor God, but it was also about honoring human life, God's creation. So when necessary he would vote, sign papers, and debate. However, he would not drive or use electricity. If there were an emergency, requiring him to get to the Capitol someone would have to drive him.

During the campaign, interviewers reminded Lieberman that Inauguration Day, January 20, 2001, would fall on the Sabbath. They asked him whether he would take the oath of office on that day. The senator answered with a quote from his mother: "Sweetheart, we should only have such a problem."

Joe Lieberman walked to the Capitol to attend the inauguration on the Sabbath. He was an observer, however, not a participant. After a very close election and five weeks of disputed votes and appeals to the courts, George W. Bush and Dick Cheney became president and vice president of the United States by a slim margin. Lieberman was reelected to the Senate, where he continued to serve Connecticut and the nation. He was proud that he had been given the opportunity to run for vice president. Because of him, more Americans of different backgrounds could be welcomed into the political arena.

TIMELINE

February 24, 1942	Joseph Isador Lieberman is born.
1964	Graduates from Yale University.
1965	Marries Betty Haas.
1966	*Power Broker* is published.
1967	Son, Matt, is born.
1967	Graduates from Yale Law School.
1969	Daughter, Rebecca, is born.
1971–81	Serves as Connecticut state senator.
1980	Loses election to the House of Representatives.
1981	Joe and Betty divorce.
1975–81	Serves as Democratic state majority leader.
1982	*The Legacy* is published.
1983	Marries Hadassah Freilich Tucker.
1983–89	Serves as Connecticut attorney general.
1988	Daughter, Hana, is born.
1989–	Serves as U.S. senator from Connecticut.
2000	Nominated for vice president as Al Gore's running mate; loses election; is reelected to U.S. Senate.

INDEX